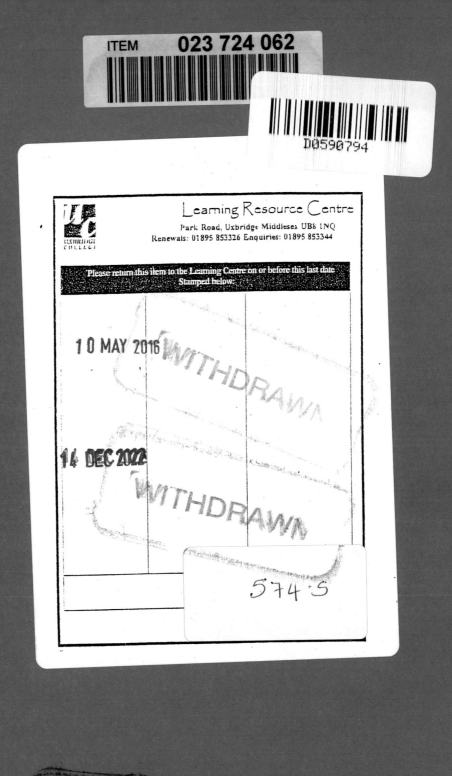

Deforestation

Richard Spilsbury

WAYLAND

First published in 2008
by Wayland
Copyright © Wayland 2008

Wayland
338 Euston Road
London NW1 3BH

Wayland Australia
Level 17/207 Kent Street
Sydney NSW 2000

Commissioning editor: Jennifer Sanderson
Designer: Jane Hawkins
Picture researcher: Kathy Lockley
Illustrator: Ian Thompson
Proofreader: Susie Brooks

Picture Acknowledgements:
The author and publisher would like to thank the following agencies for allowing these pictures to be reproduced: AFP/Getty Images: 32; Chris de Bode/Panos Pictures: 18; Rob Bowden/EASI-images: 38; Neal Cavalier-Smith/EASI-images: 24; Sue Cunningham Photographic/Alamy: 35; Digital Vision/Getty: COVER, 6, 15, 22, 29; Mark Edwards/ Still Pictures: 37; FSC: 50; Paulo Fridman/Sygma/Corbis: 27; Carlos Humberto/epa/Corbis: 31; Jacques Jangoux/; Still Pictures: 20; Ed Parker/EASI-images: 9, 10, 12, 44; Sipa Press/Rex Features: 41; Friedrich Stark/Das Fotoarchiv/Still Pictures: 16-17; USGA, photo by Lyn Topinka: 4; Tom Vezo/Still Pictures: 43

British Cataloguing in Publication Data
 Spilsbury, Richard, 1963-
   Deforestation. - (Can the earth cope?)
   1. Deforestation - Juvenile literature 2. Forest
   conservation - Juvenile literature 3. Human ecology -
   Juvenile literature
   I. Title
   333.7'5137

ISBN: 978 0 7502 5440 3

Printed in China

Wayland is a division of Hachette Children's Books,
an Hachette Livre UK company
www.hachettelivre.co.uk

Contents

Disappearing Forests

Trees first started to grow on Earth more than 300 million years ago. In parts of the planet with the right growing conditions, such as enough rain or warmth, trees formed vast forests. Over time, forest cover has changed. Forest has disappeared from some areas naturally, but the majority of deforestation has happened because of human activity. Since people first began to cut down many trees about 8,000 years ago, they have halved the world's forest cover.

Natural Deforestation

Globally, natural climate change has been a major cause of deforestation. In the past there were periods, such as ice ages, when the world's climate changed dramatically and these changes brought natural deforestation. Areas that once had the right growing conditions gradually became unsuitable for trees. For example, today Antarctica is far too cold for plants to grow, yet there are remains of trees frozen deep in the ice that prove it was once covered in tropical forest.

Evidence

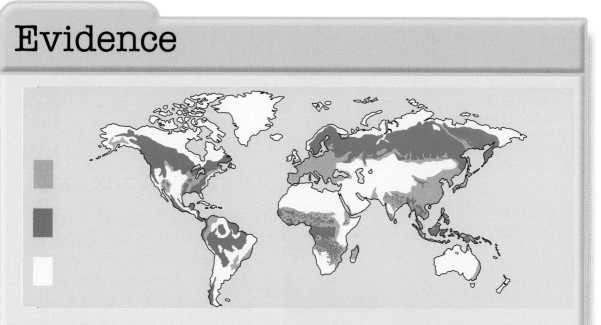

FORESTS IN THE PAST

This map shows how the area of forest around the world has changed over the last 8,000 years.

Scientists worked out the total area of forest today using aerial and satellite photography. To work out the total area of forest in the past, they used a combination of written records, old maps, and remains of trees. These include preserved wood, seeds and pollen found in soil, rock and frozen in Polar and glacier ice.

◄ This deforestation was caused by volcanic action. Forests on the slopes of Mount St Helens, Canada, were destroyed by heat and ash following a major eruption in 1986.

Natural deforestation at a more local level has other causes. For example, volcanoes may erupt hot lava or ash that knocks down and burns trees on their slopes. Lightning strikes can ignite fires that rage through forests. The spread of leaf-eating insects or tree diseases can also wipe out areas of forest.

Human Impact

People have always used trees as natural resources. For example, forests provide shelter, wood to burn for heat, and food such as nuts. However, human impact on forests has increased as the human population has grown over time. More people need to farm more land in order to grow food and they need more space in which to live. Forests often cover land people want, so they cut down the trees. Trees also provide the valuable raw materials people use to make the products they want, such as books and building materials.

The Speed of Deforestation

People have deforested land in different parts of the world at different speeds throughout history. In Europe, forests have gradually disappeared over the last 8,000 years due to land clearance for farming and building. However, in tropical areas on and near the Equator, there was little large-scale deforestation until around 500 years ago.

▼ In the Solomon Islands, in the South Pacific, a fifth of the total rainforest was destroyed between 1990 and 2005.

Rainforest Destruction

Around 500 years ago European explorers and settlers started to live in or visit Africa, South America and South-East Asia. They soon realised that tropical wood was a valuable resource that could be traded in Europe. Their ancestors, and later traders and locals, ensured that the deforestation rate increased through the subsequent centuries. Deforestation was at its worst during the 1980s and 1990s. Between 1990 and 1995, an area of forest twice the size of a football field was chopped down

IT'S A FACT

- Forests cover 27 per cent of the land area on Earth.

- 57 per cent of all forest is in less economically developed countries (LEDCs) and 43 per cent in more economically developed countries (MEDCs).

- 40 per cent of the remaining original forests are threatened by human activities.

every two seconds! In some areas the level of deforestation is immense. For example, in Africa over 80 per cent of the original tropical forest has disappeared.

Changing Rates

Today, on average, the speed of deforestation is slowing down across the globe. In some countries, such as Scotland and El Salvador, efforts to plant trees and preserve existing woodland have slowed and even reversed the decline. However, in other countries, such as Indonesia and Brazil, deforestation is continuing at high levels.

A Shared Problem

Deforestation is not the fault solely of the country where it is happening. In a global market, where countries worldwide trade with each other, the blame is shared between the countries or companies that supply forest products and those that buy them. Producers and consumers are interdependent. For example, suppose you buy a chair made from tropical forest wood from Brazil in a shop in the United Kingdom, you may be encouraging deforestation thousands of kilometres away because the shop will then need more chairs to sell and these will use up more trees.

Evidence

DEFORESTATION TOP TEN

This bar chart shows the top ten deforestation rates in the world at the start of the 21st century. Deforestation is happening fastest in Brazil, and at twice the rate of the second-placed country, Indonesia. The only MEDC on the graph is the USA.

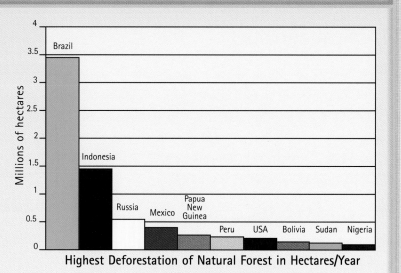

Highest Deforestation of Natural Forest in Hectares/Year

The Lowdown on Forests

The naturally occurring forests of the world are very diverse in size and in character. Each forest biome supports a particular community of plants and animals. There are four main types of forest biome: tropical, boreal, temperate and Mediterranean. Where they grow on Earth is mostly determined by climate.

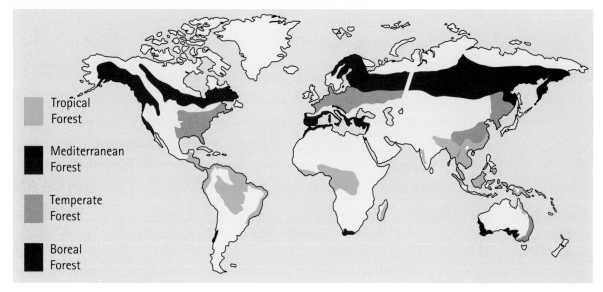

Tropical Forest

Mediterranean Forest

Temperate Forest

Boreal Forest

▲ Forests can grow only where climate supplies enough water through precipitation for trees to thrive. Different forest biomes support different tree communities.

Tropical Forests

These forests are found in the tropical parts of world, such as central Africa, South America and South-East Asia on or near the Equator. At the Equator the temperatures are high all year round and the region receives high levels of rainfall. In tropical forests the air is often very humid because the Sun's heat evaporates water rapidly. In rainforests, the humid air forms rainclouds above the trees.

Boreal Forests

These forests grow in the cold, windy regions south of the Arctic. They form a band stretching across Canada, Scandinavia and Siberia. Winters here are always long and there is little available water for trees because it is all frozen. Many boreal trees, such as firs, have small, needle-shaped leaves that help them to hold onto water in the tree. Boreal trees are usually evergreen, which means there are leaves on the trees all year around.

Temperate Forests

This biome is found in Western Europe, North-East Asia and parts of North America and contains many deciduous trees. These trees drop all of their wide leaves in autumn, partly to avoid leaf damage through the cold winter season, and then regrow new ones ready for the warm spring and summer.

Mediterranean Forests

Mediterranean forests are found south of temperate forests, for example in southern Europe, Africa and Australia. Here the climate is very hot and dry over long summers. Trees are sparse and get the water they need to grow only during the short, damp winters.

Earth's Lungs

Forests have a major impact on the Earth's atmosphere and also on its climate. Trees make food in their leaves from carbon dioxide in the air and water from their roots, using the energy in sunlight. This is called photosynthesis. During photosynthesis trees release oxygen into the atmosphere, which many living things, including people, need to breathe.

▲ The tallest trees in the world, giant redwoods, grow in temperate forests on the Pacific coast of North America.

Evidence

SUCKING UP

Trees suck up water from their roots to their leaves for photosynthesis. This suction is partly driven by transpiration. This is when water evaporates from leaf surfaces. More water then moves into the leaves through narrow tubes in the plant. This movement pulls water from the roots into the tubes. Transpiration is an effective pump of water from the soil beneath forests into the atmosphere. For example, half the rainfall in the Amazon rainforest returns to the atmosphere as a result of transpiration.

Forest Biodiversity

Forests are home to two-thirds of all land species in the world. Each biome has a typical community of living things that interact with each other, and with the non-living parts of the place in which they live, in different ways. Together they form distinct ecosystems.

Variety of Life

Boreal forests contain large areas of very few native tree species. The trees that naturally live in this biome include fir, spruce, cedar and birch. Typical boreal forest animals are wolves, bears, owls, lynxes and woodpeckers.

Tropical rainforests have incredible biodiversity, or variety of species. They cover just over 6 per cent of the Earth's surface, yet contain over 50 per cent of all the Earth's species. These forests usually have many different native tree species growing side by side. For example, more tree species have been found in a 10-hectare plot of Malaysian rainforest than the total number of native tree species in North America. Typical animals found in rainforests include sloths, parrots, hummingbirds, monkeys and insects, from butterflies to ants.

Life on a Forest Floor

Life exists at many levels in a forest, from the forest floor up to the treetop canopy. Fungi and bacteria live in the soil and amongst the roots of trees on the forest floor. These living organisms are decomposers that release nutrients from leaf litter (fallen leaves and bark), dead animals and other waste into the soil. Often, particular tree species need certain fungi species to release the nutrients they need to survive. For example, red-capped fly agaric fungi release nutrients for birch trees in exchange for sugar from the tree roots. Some animals, such as millipedes and woodlice, feed on and break up the leaf litter into pieces that the decomposers can use.

Evidence

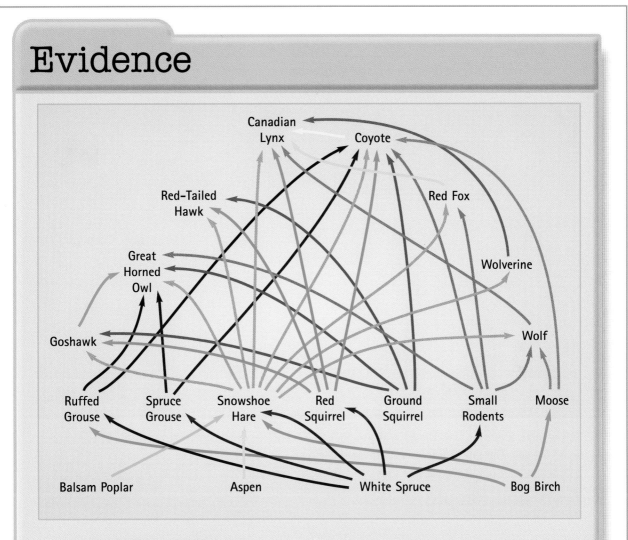

A COMPLEX BIOME

Boreal herbivores eat food from a range of tree species. This boreal food web shows the complex interdependence of the species in the biome. When trees are cut down, parts of the food web are destroyed and so many species find it difficult to find the food they need.

◀ Tree frogs are adapted for life in moist forests. Their wide, sticky fingertips help them grip onto branches and tree trunks.

Life in the Trees

Many living things spend their lives above the ground in trees. These include ferns, orchids and mosses growing on the branches, and insects living and feeding on or under tree bark. Animals, such as monkeys and gibbons, use their long arms and acrobatic skills to travel through the canopy in search of the leaves and fruits they like to eat.

▲ This woman is cutting into the bark of a rubber tree to release the sap. The sap is processed to make rubber.

Forests and People

People harvest a wide range of products from forests. The most obvious are timber products, including wood for construction and wood pulp. Wood pulp is ground-up wood used for making paper and the absorbent part of disposable nappies. People harvest products other than timber from forest trees, including sap, which is used to make rubber, and nuts.

For many people in MEDCs, forests are places of recreation where they go to hike, bike, fish and picnic. For many people in LEDCs, forests are spaces where their herds of animals can graze. For some indigenous people, such as the mbuti or pygmy people of central Africa, forests provide most of their food and plants to make traditional medicines.

IT'S A FACT

• Non-timber forest products (NTFPs) are vital natural resources for many poor people around the world.

• NTFPs include fuelwood burnt to cook food and heat homes, and forest foods, such as honey from wild bees.

• Around 80 per cent of people in LEDCs rely on NTFPs for subsistence. Without these free materials to use or sell, their lives would be much more difficult.

Supplying Water, Protecting Land

All forests help to trap and supply water. Tree roots hold the soil together and this, with the leaf litter, soaks up and stores rainwater rather like a sponge. The forest floor gradually releases water, which trickles into streams, rivers, lakes, reservoirs and groundwater supplies. Water is vital for all living things to survive and it is easier to get water from regularly topped-up water sources. Many communities worldwide have established and rely upon the stable water sources controlled by forests.

Forests also prevent problems caused by heavy rains. For example, trees growing on slopes help to prevent rapid run-off of water that could cause flooding. Their roots hold soil together so it is less likely to slip down slopes when it is heavy and water-soaked.

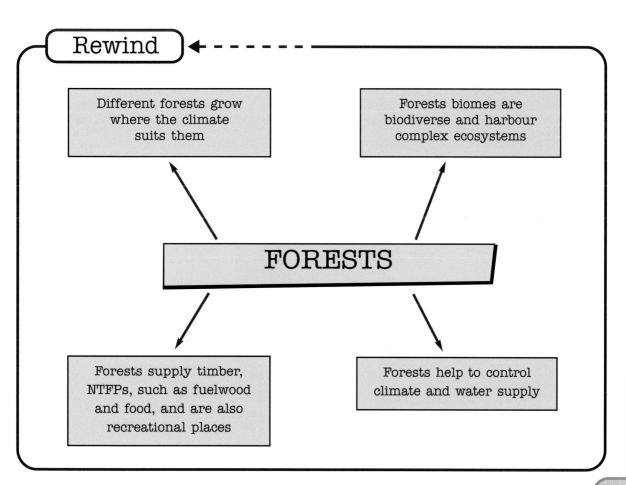

Rewind

Different forests grow where the climate suits them

Forests biomes are biodiverse and harbour complex ecosystems

FORESTS

Forests supply timber, NTFPs, such as fuelwood and food, and are also recreational places

Forests help to control climate and water supply

What Causes Deforestation?

People cut down trees for two main resources; timber and land. The cleared land is used for a wide range of activities from farming to mining. People are frequently driven to deforestation by poverty.

Logging

The felling of trees so that their wood can be sold is called logging. Logging is a massive industry worldwide because wood is a highly valued raw material. It is very strong for its weight yet it can also bend. Wood is fairly easily sawn, shaped and processed into the sizes and shapes needed.

Logging is generally carried out by teams of people with large chainsaws and powerful vehicles for lifting and removing the logs. Loggers may cut down all of the trees in a large area, which is called

Evidence

THE PRICE OF TIMBER

The price people pay for timber depends on several factors. Most important of these is availability: rare hardwoods such as teak cost more than plantation-grown spruce. Another factor is transport: wood costs more if it has to be shipped from further away. A third factor is processing: wood that is sawn into neat pieces costs more than whole logs per cubic metre because time has been spent and machinery used to process it.

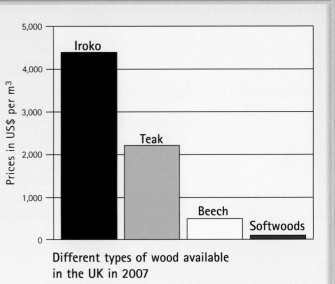

Different types of wood available in the UK in 2007

clearfelling, or they may clear strips separated by forest. However, they may also be more selective about picking the largest or most valuable trees. Logs are processed in machines on site, or in factories elsewhere, into sawn timber, wood chips or pulp.

Softwoods and Hardwoods

Wood is generally divided into two kinds. Softwoods come from fast-growing conifers, such as pine, fir and hemlock, that grow in boreal forests. They are important for construction and are easier to process than hardwoods such as oak or teak. Hardwoods generally come from slow-growing, broad-leaved trees in temperate or tropical forests. Hardwoods are often more decorative than softwoods and rot more slowly. They are used to make fine furniture, window frames and floors, and also sheet building materials such as plywood.

▲ A huge hardwood tree trunk is cut down with a chainsaw in the Philippines.

A Renewable Resource

Wood is a renewable resource. When adult trees are cut down, their seeds in the soil can grow into new trees to take their places. However, this natural process does not always happen, for example because animals eat the seeds, and it also takes a long time. A softwood tree takes about 30 years to reach full size but many hardwood species can take twice or even three times that. People around the world help this process by planting seedling trees in plantations. These are areas planted and managed to provide a continuous crop by growing new plants as others are used up. Softwood plantations are the source of all wood pulp used to make new paper and cardboard.

Meeting the Demand

The demand for timber, especially hardwoods, is very high. Many governments decide on a balance between conserving forest biomes in their countries and making money from selling timber. They allocate certain areas where logging companies can legally cut down trees in exchange for payment, and they protect other areas from deforestation.

Illegal Logging

However, most logging around the world happens illegally in protected forests in every forest biome, from tropical to boreal. It happens not just in LEDCs, such as Brazil and Cameroon, but also in MEDCs, such as Canada, Bulgaria and Russia. Illegal loggers often target ancient forests that are protected. These forests have had decades or centuries without disturbance, so the trees are tall. Loggers often clearfell large areas with bulldozers to get to valuable trees that they can sell for more money than the smaller ones. Much of the demand for illegal logging comes from MEDCs, where people use large amounts of wood products.

IT'S A FACT

- 83 per cent of all timber from Indonesia and 45 per cent from Bulgaria comes from illegal logging.

- The European Union buys wood and wood products sourced illegally worth around US$6 billion each year.

- Nearly one-tenth of timber imports into Australia are the result of illegal logging in Asia Pacific countries nearby.

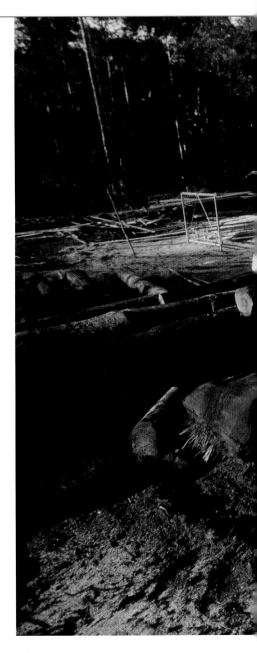

▲ Logging in the Paradise Forest of Papua New Guinea is destroying not only the habitat, but also the traditions and lives of local people who live in the forest.

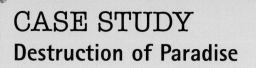

CASE STUDY
Destruction of Paradise

The Paradise Forest of Papua New Guinea is home to many different indigenous peoples who rely on forest foods and shelter for their survival. Many rare plant and animal species can also be found in the forest. These include tree kangaroos, Queen Alexandra's birdwings, which are the largest butterflies on Earth, and rosewood trees.

Paradise is being destroyed through illegal and destructive logging by foreign companies. Some of the timber ends up in Australia as garden furniture and a lot is bought by China. In China, factories make sheets of plywood by cutting the logs into thin sheets that they glue together. This tough, flexible material is then sold worldwide to countries such as the United Kingdom.

Brian Baring of the Borong people who live in the forest says, "Without the forests we have nothing. It is like our supermarket, our pharmacy, our building centre. Our everything. Imagine if someone bulldozed down the shops that supply your daily needs and sold everything on their shelves to someone in a country on the other side of the world. How would you feel?"

Subsistence Farming

Many individual families and communities around the world clear small areas of forest to create smallholdings. They have gardens where they can grow vegetables and fruit or keep animals. However, this impact is minor in comparison with large-scale deforestation for farming. Each year, an area twice the size of Paris, France, is converted to farmland.

Cash Crops

Most of the deforestation in Asia is to farm crops, such as palm oil, which people can sell for cash. Oil palms produce fat-filled fruit and this fat is used in many things, from ice-creams and bread to shower gel and lipstick. Other major cash crops include soy beans that are used to make oil and various foods, coffee, and fast-growing woods, such as eucalyptus and acacia. These woods are usually pulped to make cheap paper.

▼ A woman preparing her field for a peanut crop in a deforested part of Madagascar.

Cattle Ranching

In Central and South America around two-thirds of all deforestation is to create grassland for cattle ranching. Ranchers clear trees to plant grasses that thrive in the tropical conditions and that can support the large numbers of cattle that live on the ranches. The cattle provide meat and meat products, such as beefburgers and pet food.

Evidence

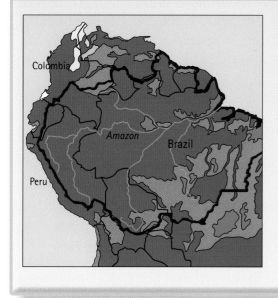

NOTORIOUS RANCHES

The area of land used for cattle ranching in South America is increasing each year. The orange areas on this map show where forest surrounding the Amazon is threatened by cattle ranching. The demand for ranch space is partly the result of Brazilian beef being cheaper than beef raised in the USA and Europe. However, it comes at a cost to the rainforest. Cattle need lots of pasture to graze and for every hamburger made from rainforest beef that is consumed in the USA, about 16 square metres of rainforest has been cleared.

Overseas Demand

Much of the demand to convert forest to farmland in LEDCs comes from MEDCs. For example, palm oil and meat from tropical places are cheaper for MEDCs to import than locally grown alternatives. Some people argue that foods grown on deforested land help feed an ever-increasing world population and that cash crops give people in LEDCs vital money. However, others believe that less destructive farming practices can provide the food people need. They also argue that more money from land conversion goes to the rich traders and companies who deal with cash crops, than to the poor people who live in forest regions.

CASE STUDY
Biofuels and Deforestation

People are looking to alternatives to petrol and diesel to power their cars. This is because burning these fuels releases greenhouse gases that can cause climate change. Oil prices worldwide are rising as stocks run dry so people also want cheaper alternatives to petrol and diesel. One such alternative is ethanol, which is made by processing sugar cane or maize.

A growing area of land in the Brazilian rainforest is being clearfelled each year to plant sugar cane to make into ethanol. Prices for ethanol are rising so much that some farmers in the USA are no longer growing soy beans but are planting maize instead. This is in turn pushing up soy prices worldwide, so more Brazilian farmers are clearing forest to plant soy.

Mines

Another major cause of deforestation is the development of mines. The rocks underneath tropical forests sometimes contain reserves of valuable metals such as copper and gold, and gemstones such as rubies. Miners use heavy machinery to clear forests, and explosives and powerful pumps to clear away rock and soil. Sometimes more trees are destroyed to make fuel to process what is mined. For example, Carajas iron ore mine in Brazil used vast amounts of fuelwood to extract iron from the ore before it had established plantations to provide its own fuel.

Powerplants and Pipelines

Power industries include not only hydroelectric powerplants, but also new oil fields. In remote forest areas, hydroelectric plants are important ways of creating electricity to power local industry and to provide people with electric light and other amenities. Hydroelectric (HEP) schemes usually involve building dams across forest rivers to create reservoirs. Deep water from the reservoirs flows through turbines to create cleaner electricity than that made by coal, gas or oil-fired powerplants. However, reservoirs can flood large areas of forest, transforming biomes. Oil is a vital source of income for any country and is also used for fuels and in industry to make materials, such as plastics.

◄ Trucks at Carajas iron mine in Brazil shift 1 million tons of earth each day to extract iron ore.

Digging oil fields may involve little direct deforestation. However, both powerplants and oil fields usually require long powerlines or pipelines to carry the electricity or oil to where it is needed. People may clear vast corridors of trees for these lines to make them easy to maintain.

Access to the Forest

The development of logging and mining industries in forests often brings new roads to transport logs and mined materials. More forest is cleared for settlements where workers in these industries can live. Secondary roads develop from main roads and gradually forested areas are criss-crossed with human development. Roads through forests are important routes for transporting goods by lorry to and from settlements. Building roads does not cause much deforestation directly, but it increases access to the forest. Service industries, such as restaurants, shops and lodges, and farms or ranches, develop in the cleared land around roads.

Evidence

THREATENED FRONTIERS

Scientists looking at forests around the world have identified 40 per cent as frontier forests. These are forests whose ecosystems are largely unaffected by people and contain a mix of native trees of different ages and rich biodiversity. They are typical of their biome. Half of all frontier forests are boreal and over one-third of all frontier forests are threatened with deforestation. This bar chart shows the threats to frontier forests worldwide and reveals that mining and power industries are second to logging in threatening forests.

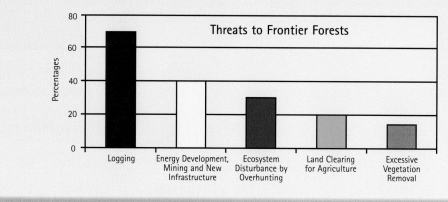

Threats to Frontier Forests

Percentages (y-axis: 0, 20, 40, 60, 80)

Logging | Energy Development, Mining and New Infrastructure | Ecosystem Disturbance by Overhunting | Land Clearing for Agriculture | Excessive Vegetation Removal

Forest Fires

Forest fires are a natural cause of deforestation in some forest biomes, such as Mediterranean and boreal forests. In some cases, fires can benefit the long-term health of forests by killing off dead trees and clearing space for seedlings to grow. Some tree species, such as Banksia, which is found in Australian woodland, can grow only from partially burnt seeds. When the wood burns, it forms ash and the nutrients in ash wash into the soil, making it more fertile. However, every year, hundreds of thousands of square kilometres of forests are destroyed because people set them alight.

Slash-and-Burn Deforestation

Many forest fires begin accidentally as a result of slash-and-burn farming. This is when farmers cut down forest and then light small fires to clear the land of the remaining stumps and waste. These fires then spread to surrounding forest. However, sometimes people who want to start plantations, for example of oil palms, may start fires to clear forest quickly. This was the cause of a fire that raged for more than six months in Indonesia in 1997/1998, affecting an area of forest the size of the United Kingdom.

▼ Fires can move quickly through forests, destroying most of the plant and animal life in large areas.

IT'S A FACT

- 1 per cent of world forest cover, which is an area the size of New Zealand, burns each year.

- 95 per cent of forest fires in the Mediterranean are started by people.

- There are about 15,000 forest fires in Australia every year.

Global Warming

Most scientists agree that the world's climate is changing as a result of human action and this has an effect on forests. When people burn fuels in vehicles and powerplants, carbon dioxide and other gases rise into the air. These gases can absorb and trap heat in the atmosphere in a process called the greenhouse effect. In some parts of the world, the climate is becoming warmer. Warmer air and drier trees create ideal conditions for forest fires. The hotter climate also means that insect pests can spread into new areas that previously were not warm enough for them.

Acid Rain Pollution

Deforestation is also caused by acid rain. Burning fuels in powerplants and factories release polluting gases, such as sulphur dioxide and nitrogen dioxide, into the atmosphere. The gases mix with water vapour and form droplets of weak acid in clouds in the sky. When this acidic water falls to Earth as precipitation, it damages and even kills trees.

Evidence

HOW ACID RAIN KILLS TREES

Acid rain usually falls on forests downwind of factories creating a lot of air pollution. For example, areas of the Canadian boreal forest are affected by pollution from US factories. Acid rain can scar leaf surfaces directly but its biggest effect is on nutrients found in the soil.

A. Acid and nutrients such as magnesium and potassium in rain fall on a tree.
B. Chemicals in acid take the place of nutrients in soil. Water washes away, or leaches, more nutrients from the soil. The tree has fewer nutrients to take up and gets sick. Its leaves turn yellow so it cannot make food.

Poverty

Poverty is a driving force behind global deforestation. Worldwide nearly one billion people live in or around tropical forests and woodlands. Many of these people are extremely poor and depend heavily on the forest for much of their food, fuel and income. In Malawi, for example, nearly two-thirds of the population are so poor that they cannot afford to meet their basic needs. About 90 per cent of these people live in rural areas amongst patchy forests. About 40 per cent of all the wood taken from global forests is used as fuelwood. Poor people have no other options for domestic energy sources as they cannot afford more expensive fuels, such as oil, and often have no access to electricity.

Many people in LEDCs cannot afford to buy food, so they must farm or find what they need themselves. They need to farm whatever land is available, forested or not. They might welcome the chance to earn a wage from a job in logging (legal or illegal) or on a plantation. They may not be well educated owing to a lack of money and time for schooling. For example, in countries such as India or Nepal it is often the children who collect fuelwood.

Hours spent harvesting fuelwood are a constant in the daily lives of poor people, including children, in LEDCs.

Children may spend over two hours each day collecting wood, in addition to time spent helping in the home or on farms. This is time that they could use study or to get to school. Where trees are one of the only free resources available, it is difficult for poor people to balance their own needs for survival with the importance of preserving forest biomes.

Forced to Move

Political situations can force the movement of people into forested areas and increase deforestation. For example, at one point during the civil war in Rwanda in the early 1990s, 850,000 homeless people moved into the rainforests of the Virunga National Park. They deforested 300 square kilometres of frontier forest in their search for food and fuelwood.

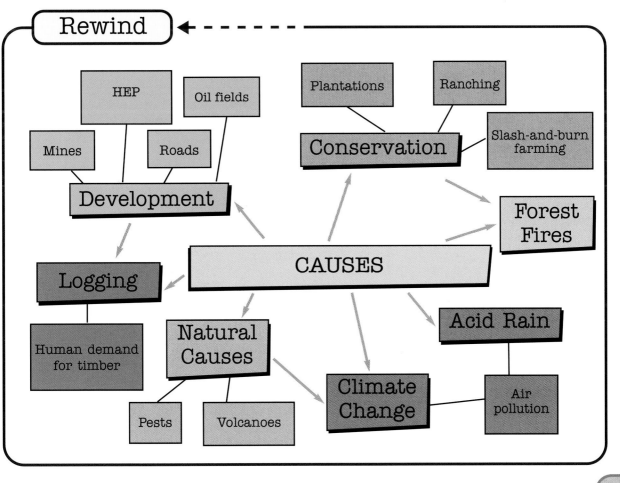

Rewind

HEP
Oil fields
Mines
Roads
Development

Plantations
Ranching
Conservation
Slash-and-burn farming

Forest Fires

CAUSES

Logging
Human demand for timber

Natural Causes
Pests
Volcanoes

Acid Rain
Air pollution

Climate Change

The Impact of Deforestation

Deforestation can dramatically change landscapes in a short time. However, the effects of deforestation may last for years. The changes in landscape range from local loss of biodiversity to large-scale effects on ecosystems and the atmosphere.

Loss of Wildlife Habitat

For many animals, the forest is their natural habitat. When trees are cut down, this reduces the space, food and other resources available to the wild animals who live in forest biomes. The danger of species becoming extinct, or completely wiped out, is especially high in the species-rich tropical forest biome (see page 8). For example, most parrots live in tropical forests, feed on forest fruits and nest in holes in trees. Without trees they cannot survive. Deforestation is a major reason why nearly a third of parrot species worldwide are endangered.

Evidence

FOREST RICHNESS

Surveys of the Malaysian rainforest have compared the proportion of mammal species in different categories of forest. They have found that the more a forest is disturbed by people, the fewer the species that live there.

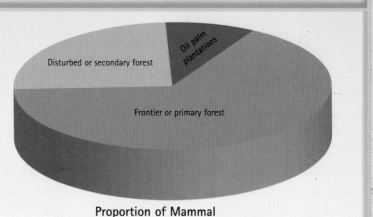

Disturbed or secondary forest

Oil palm plantations

Frontier or primary forest

Proportion of Mammal Species in Catagories of Forest

▲ Wide roads through forests fragment the habitat for wildlife and increase pressure on forests by people.

Forest Fragmentation

Problems for forest species are made worse by the construction of roads, plantations and settlements. Populations of animals and plants may become isolated from each other in small fragments of forest. Parrots, for example, cannot fly long distances, so habitat fragmentation reduces the chance of their finding other parrots with which to breed. As a result, tree species that rely on parrots or other animals to spread their seeds, so that they can grow in other places, may not survive. When large forest animals, such as tigers and elephants, become trapped in a fragment of forest, unable to move elsewhere because of roads or settlements, they may not have the space they need to find sufficient food.

The Wrong Type of Habitat

Deforestation is not always straightforward. In some places, such as Canada, China and Scandinavia there is no overall reduction in forest area. However, frontier forests are being replaced with new plantations. Generally, plantations are not good habitats for wildlife. This is because they are planted with one species of plant, and chemicals are used on the crop to reduce pests and prevent other plants from growing in spaces between them. This keeps away many types of wildlife. Over 700 animals species, including lynx, flying squirrels and forest reindeer, are endangered in Finland following conversion of old frontier forests into new plantations.

Knock-on Effects

As forests become smaller and roads are built deeper into the forests, hunters are able to find more wild animals. For example, several African primates such as chimpanzees and gorillas are now endangered because of the growing trade in bushmeat. This is meat from wild animals that is highly prized in some cultures. Some hunters also catch forest animals for sale as pets. However, it is not just animals that suffer, some plants are now endangered because they are taken from forests by plant collectors and sold in garden centres. These include tree ferns from New Zealand and orchids from tropical rainforests.

People Problems

Deforestation also leads to increased conflict between people and forest animals. For example, forest elephants damage crops in their search for enough food, so people try to kill elephants. When settlers move onto deforested land, they bring in cultures and influences that can change the lives of indigenous forest people.

Deforestation removes forest plants that indigenous people use as medicines. It also reduces the bank of plant species that could be useful as medicines for people in the future.

Evidence

RAINFOREST DRUGS

Various chemicals give natural protection to rainforest plants against attack by forest insects and disease. Some of the chemicals are used to make drugs that treat diseases. For example, scientists at the US National Cancer Institute have identified over 3,000 plants containing chemicals that are active against cancer and about 70 per cent of these are found only in rainforests. Here are a few of the drugs from the rainforest that are used worldwide:

DRUG	ORIGIN	USE
Quinine	Cinchona tree (South America)	Treats malaria
Novacaine	Coca plant (South America)	Local anaesthetic
Turbocuarine	Liana vine (USA)	Muscle relaxant
Vincristine	Rosy periwinkle (Madagascar)	Treats cancers

CASE STUDY
Palm Oil and Orangutans

Palm oil fruit is the most widely grown fruit in the world. It is a popular crop because each tree produces lots of fruit and each fruit has a high yield of oil. People have deforested Indonesia since the mid–1960s to make palm oil plantations. This increase in oil palm crops is the major reason why orangutans are becoming rarer.

Orangutans are rare primates that live only in the Indonesian rainforest. To make a plantation, trees are logged and then the remaining stumps are removed by slash-and-burn. Burning kills orangutans because they are slow-moving and cannot escape the flames. Farmers sometimes shoot adult orangutans because they are considered to be pests. They also shoot or trap adults so that they can capture the young. Baby orangutans are sought-after

pets in Indonesia. When young, they are cute but they soon become too big to handle as they grow up. As a result, many pet orangutans are neglected and die in captivity. Those that are abandoned cannot care for themselves in the remaining forest. In parts of Indonesia, there are conservation centres where people care for orphan orangutans.

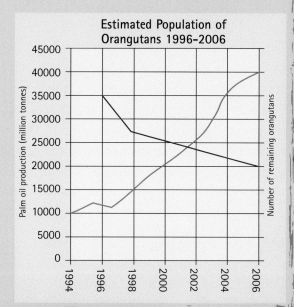

Land Degradation

Deforestation can degrade the land beneath the trees. Without tree roots, the topsoil is exposed to rain that can wash it away. Topsoil contains more nutrients than soil deeper underground so when topsoil becomes eroded, the remaining soil is less fertile.

Hard Soil

The soil layers exposed by erosion can dry in the Sun. Layers, called laterite, in tropical rainforest soil contain metal minerals, such as iron, which set as hard as rock. The hardening effect is worse when the soil is compacted by bulldozers and by the movement of cattle across ranches. Heavy rain cannot soak into the hardened soil and instead causes flash floods that can wash away anything including topsoil, roads, bridges and even whole communities.

Water Problems

Deforestation can also cause water shortages in forests. Fast-growing plantation trees, such as acacia, use up water faster than forest plant species. When topsoil washes down a river from farmland, the nutrients in the water can cause rapid growth in tiny water plants. These can make the water unsuitable for animals to live in.

Deforestation pollutes rivers in different ways. Pesticides used on plantations may wash off the soil into rivers and lakes. Industries that use machinery in forests can create spills of oil and chemicals. For example, mining for gold uses the toxic metal mercury to help extract gold. The mercury accumulates through forest river food webs and animals may become sick because they eat other animals that contain some mercury.

Evidence

SLASH-AND-BURN DEGRADATION

After farmers slash and burn rainforest to grow crops, the farmland is productive for only up to three years. Tropical trees often retain a lot of nutrients compared with the soil in which they grow. Some of these nutrients are lost when the trees are burned or removed. Although farmers add the ash from burning to enrich the soil, most of the nutrients are washed away by rainfall. This graph shows how the crop yield of corn grown on cleared rainforest land drops year by year after slash and burn. As the yield falls, rainforest plants start to grow and take over the farm once more. Given a choice farmers will usually slash and burn new areas of forest rather than try to use the exhausted land beyond the third year.

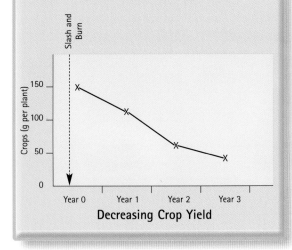

CASE STUDY
Road to Ruin

In the 1970s, the Brazilian government started a 3,000-kilometre highway through the centre of the massive Amazon rainforest. Its aim was to open forest land to poor farmers from north Brazil and to developers of timber and mineral resources and cattle ranches. The government encouraged settlers to move into the region by giving out pieces of land to clear and money to help start farming.

The Trans-Amazonian Highway project had problems from the start. There was massive erosion of as much as 100 tonnes of soil per hectare after clearing. Some of the soil washed onto the highway, blocking traffic and burying crops so they were ruined and left to rot. Harvests for the new farmers were poor because forest soils quickly became infertile. Logging was difficult because the valuable trees loggers wanted were dotted over wide areas of forest.

There are many indigenous people living in the Amazon. One of the largest groups of the Yanomani people live in the Roraima territory. Part of the highway crossed their territory and, as a result, construction workers and other settlers passed on diseases, including measles and tuberculosis, to the Yanomani. The Yanomani had not encountered the diseases before and hundreds of them died. Many Yanomani abandoned their traditional lives by turning to begging, hitchhiking to construction sites and living in roadside shacks rather than tribal villages.

Global Warming

Many scientists believe that removing trees from Earth is causing global warming. Earth temperatures are mediated by the greenhouse effect. This is when gases such as carbon dioxide in the atmosphere trap heat from sunlight reflected off the Earth's surface. The balance of carbon dioxide is maintained by green plants, which absorb the gas to create their own food by photosynthesis. Global warming is happening because large amounts of greenhouse gases are entering the atmosphere. Most are produced as a result of burning fuels but some are caused by deforestation.

Slash-and-burn agriculture and forest fires associated with deforestation also release carbon dioxide. Other greenhouse gases in the atmosphere, such as methane, are also increasing following deforestation. Methane absorbs much more heat than carbon dioxide, so has a greater greenhouse effect. Methane is released into the air from the stomachs of plant-eating cattle ranched on deforested land. Methane is also created, for example, when plants rot after forest is flooded for HEP schemes. But a much greater effect of deforestation is that there are fewer trees to absorb carbon dioxide.

▼ Rainforests in Indonesia, where tigers once roamed, are being cleared for land to create acacia plantations. Acacia is a quick-growing wood used to make timber products.

Global warming is not just about rising temperatures. Warming also increases evaporation of surface water in some places, creating more rainfall. In addition, it also creates bigger temperature differences in air masses over different areas of land. This produces air pressure differences, which cause strong winds to blow. Deforestation can reduce local rainfall because more water runs off land and less is transpired through trees into the air, forming fewer rainclouds.

Helping the Atmosphere?

Some people say that plantations of young trees may help the atmosphere more than old trees in forests. This is because plants absorb carbon dioxide faster when they are young. However, other people argue that old trees are a massive store of carbon in the form of wood. This 'carbon bank' takes decades or centuries to build up. When they are logged or burnt to clear land for plantations, the carbon released by old trees as carbon dioxide far exceeds that which is absorbed by plantation trees. The difference between how much carbon is absorbed by plantation trees and that released by disappearing frontier forest cover is especially acute in the giant plantations of the boreal forests.

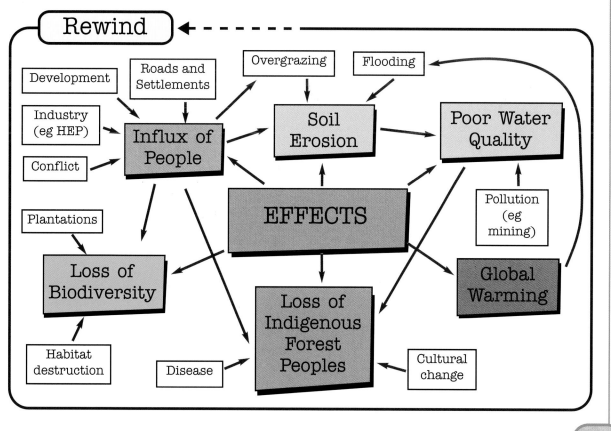

Sustainable Solutions

The obvious solution to deforestation is to stop cutting down trees and to preserve the remaining forests. However, forests and the land they cover are a vital natural resource that many people want or need to use. The difficulty lies in making the use of forest biomes sustainable.

Forest Conservation

Reserves are areas of forest that are guarded. Governments use barriers, rangers and punishments, ranging from fines to imprisonment, to control who goes in and what is taken out of reserves. In 2007, 12 per cent of the world's total forest area was protected, an area half the size of the USA. However, in many places conservation is in trouble. For example, rangers are too thinly spread over large areas or are poorly equipped to stop illegal logging and other forest abuses. In Brazil, there are typically just 50 rangers for an area the size of France. Many rangers are poorly paid and may easily be bribed to allow illegal logging.

Evidence

PROTECTED FOREST

The red areas on this world map show protected forests. North and Central America are the regions with most protected forest, each protecting around one-fifth of their forests. In Europe only one in twenty of forests are protected. Compare this map with the one on page 8 showing forest biomes, and you can see that more species-rich tropical forest is being conserved than boreal forest.

Conservation Value

It is important to use the money spent on conservation as effectively as possible. That is why many conservation charities, such as WWF, and governments of countries with forest biomes are focusing their efforts on protecting high conservation value forests (HCVFs). These include frontier forests or especially rare forest biomes such as mountain forests, with unusual or rich biodiversity. Conservationists say that it is more important to conserve these areas than forest that has already been altered and partly spoilt by people. Some conservation efforts focus on maintaining narrow corridors of forest between reserves so that animals can move between them. Such forest corridors have been effective, for example, in India by linking protected areas where elephants live.

▶ A powered airship carries forest researchers into the canopy to study life high in the rainforest trees.

CASE STUDY
Gola Forest

A new rainforest national park has been created in Senegal. It is one of the remaining sections of a forest biome that once stretched right across West Africa. The park will employ 100 people to look after an area of 750 square kilometres. The reserve will protect a unique ecosystem of over 300 species of bird, including the rufous fishing owl, 50 mammal species, including the rare pygmy hippo and red colobus monkeys, and nearly 600 different species of butterfly.

Sustainable Forestry

People will always need to harvest wood and other forest products. Sustainable forestry does this without ruining forest biomes. It can create better plantations to supply both cash crops and locally important resources, such as fuelwood. When the plantations mix crops with native trees and other local plants, they are not only more biodiverse than single-species plantations, but also suffer less soil erosion and develop more fertile soil. Encouraging local species of animals into plantations can also be beneficial. For example, some insects may naturally defend crops from pests without the need for expensive insecticides.

Managing Forests

Forest can also be managed to make them more productive. For example, poor, stunted trees may be cleared to make space for bigger specimens. New, native trees can be planted to replace those logged and logging itself can be done with lower impact on forests. For example, using portable sawmills to reduce soil damage caused by heavy vehicles bringing logs to permanent sites. However, foresters argue that this approach takes longer and becomes less cost-effective.

Evidence

CHANGING FORESTS

Worldwide there are changes in forest cover each year. This map shows the change in forests in 2005. The green areas mark regions where the area of forest is increasing each year and the pink areas where it is decreasing. The grey areas are where replanting, usually in plantations, balances deforestation.

Reversing Deforestation

Reforestation of already deforested land ranges from local initiatives, such as tree planting in local parks, to national movements to create large forests, such as those in China (see case study below). However, reforestation can happen naturally given time. In tropical areas, secondary forest grows in clearings surrounded by forest within a decade. Although the secondary forest will be less biodiverse and younger than the original forest, it will still be adequate for some species to return.

▶ A child in Burkina Faso waters a young tree she has just planted as part of a village reforestation project.

CASE STUDY
Reforestation for Water

In 2002, the Chinese government began the biggest reforestation project. The government plans to plant trees across 5 per cent of the country – that is an area the size of California, USA. There are several aims for the project. By planting trees the government hopes the tree roots will help to slow the soil erosion that has caused disastrous droughts and regular dust storms in recent years. Water shortage is a growing problem in parts of China owing to drying land and soil degradation as a result of intensive farming to grow food. The stabilised soil should absorb rainfall better and replenish water resources. The plan will also create forest reserves where rare species such as giant pandas and unusual orchids can thrive.

Sustainable Development

Communities are more likely to manage forest areas sustainably, so that they remain in good condition for future generations, when they are are educated about what forests can do for them. A community forest, which is a forest maintained by a group of people for shared resources, ensures a steady supply of fuelwood, timber, forest foods and other products for use or sale over the long term. It also conserves biodiversity, keeps water clean and safeguards the local environment. By educating communities, people will realise that forest destruction may bring more money in the short term, but also delivers long-term problems.

Changing Practices

Communities that own areas of forest or live in reserves can change the way they farm to look after the forest. For example, rainforest farmers may change from slash-and-burn farming to permaculture.

▲ These ecotourists are learning about life in the Mabira Forest, Uganda, from a local forest guide. The money they pay to visit helps the Mabira community to conserve the rainforest.

This is where they grow plants to increase the natural fertility of the soil and use the same fields time after time. Farmers may also grow high-value cash crops, such as brazil nuts or cocoa beans, that thrive in secondary forest. They can also develop small-scale fish farming. For example, in the Amazon, some farmers keep large, high-value arapaima fish in ponds in the forest. This ensures a supply of protein food for forest communities and for sale elsewhere.

Diversification

Forest people are finding new ways to earn money from forests by encouraging ecotourism. Ecotourism is small-scale, sustainable tourism, which uses a minimum of resources, such as water, helps to conserve biomes and provides jobs for local people.

Another way to make forests pay is by sustainably developing and selling their bioresources. These are the raw materials from living things that people want to use, for example to make drugs. The drug company Merck paid US$1 million to study plants in Costa Rica's forests for useful medicines. If the company sells drugs using what it finds, it will pay Costa Rica more to set up conservation projects.

CASE STUDY
Ecotourism in Costa Rica

Costa Rica in Central America has a fast-growing ecotourism industry with 6 per cent more visitors each year. The number of reserves is growing so more forest is protected. However, its success is bringing problems, such as increasing environmental damage. For example, one of Costa Rica's most popular parks, Manuel Antonio, receives as many as 1,000 visitors every day. These visitors damage the forest floor and often drop litter. Some local monkeys now feed only on rubbish. Although most hotels in Costa Rica are small scale, a massive new hotel development at Papagayo is being built to accommodate extra tourists. The hotel is paid for and will be owned and run by people from other countries. Such foreign investment is likely to take more tourism money out of the country and not benefit local people.

Changing Timber Habits

When many people buy timber or NTFPs, they want to be sure that it does not come from illegally logged sources that damage forests. Many wood products have certification labels, such as Forest Stewardship Council (FSC) or Treemark, which mean that the wood is produced legally and sustainably from managed forests.

▲ When you see this mark on timber or NTFPs there is a guarantee that the wood is from sustainable sources.

Another way to help forests is to use less wood by buying second-hand furniture and recycling paper so that fewer trees are felled to make woodpulp. Although this takes away business from timber producers, it provides work in the recycling industry.

Using the Law

Many governments use laws to protect their forests. In 2004, Paraguay made it illegal to convert forest into farmland and then regularly checked satellite images of its forests to find and punish law breakers. By 2006, deforestation was reduced by 85 per cent in parts of the country. The difficulty in using the law is that often it is the poor people cutting down the trees who are punished, although rich traders may actually be responsible for the demand.

International Agreements

Some countries sign up to international agreements preventing the trade of illegally logged wood and rare tree species, such as mahogany. It is in the interests of any country with forest resources to sign up. This is because an estimated US$12 billion is lost from legal logging companies and governments globally each year to illegal logging criminals. Charities such as WWF and Friends of the Earth, play an important role by encouraging governments to agree on guarding forests. These charities study forests, the effects of deforestation, and their campaigners raise awareness of the issues in the media so people know all about it. Then people ask their governments to look after forests better.

The fair trade movement can also help forests. It makes sure farmers of NTFPs such as brazil nuts and spices get a fair price for their goods so they do not have to resort to slash-and-burn farming and other deforestation.

IT'S A FACT

- Three per cent of all forest area is certified by FSC.
- Recycling 1 tonne of paper saves 17 trees.
- WWF started the first campaign to save tropical rainforests in 1975.

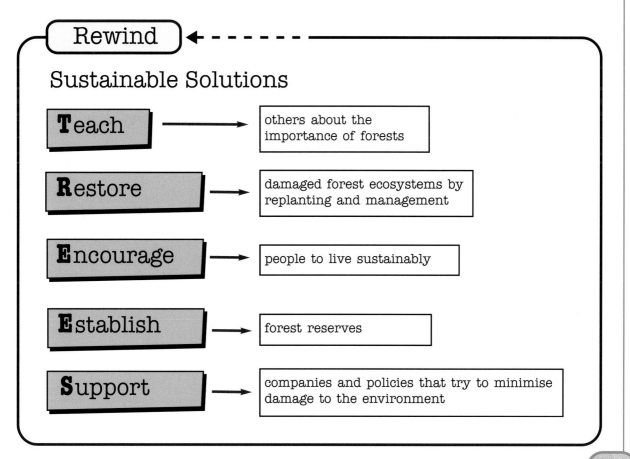

An environmental group protests about deforestation to make space for a building project by occupying a tree planned for felling. Protests such as these publicise environmental threats and may encourage decision-makers to conserve woodland.

Rewind

Sustainable Solutions

Teach ⟶ others about the importance of forests

Restore ⟶ damaged forest ecosystems by replanting and management

Encourage ⟶ people to live sustainably

Establish ⟶ forest reserves

Support ⟶ companies and policies that try to minimise damage to the environment

Making Sure the Earth Copes

The Earth is at a critical point in its long history. Forests are essential for its health. If people continue to destroy forests at the present rate, the planet will not be able to cope. People can make sure the Earth copes for future generations if they make some major changes in how they care for its biomes. Imagine how different the possible and preferable futures could be.

A Possible Future

If rainforest destruction continues at the current rate, both the quantity and the quality of forest will be affected. The total area of natural forest will dwindle. For example, tropical African forest will shrink by half. Frontier forest will probably disappear completely, so that all remaining forest will be secondary, degraded and patchy.

Evidence

DISAPPEARING RAINFOREST

Scientists have predicted how the world's tropical rainforest will continue to shrink at the present rates of deforestation. In 2000, the area of forest was half that in 1940. Since 2000, the rate of loss has reduced relative to the previous decades. However, even this reduced deforestation will be sufficient to take the rainforests to the brink of survival. The scientists place the end of rainforests at some point between 2030 and 2040.

Scientists predict that, through fragmentation and habitat loss, many rare animals such as tigers and orangutans may well become extinct in the wild. Rare tree species such as mahogany will also become extinct. The ways of life of indigenous forest peoples may wiped out.

Resource Demand

Deforestation may be difficult to stop because of the world demand for forest resources. Demand for cheap food, such as ranched meat and soy beans, grown on tropical plantations will drive further Amazon deforestation. For example, China is funding the creation of a new road from the Amazon to the Pacific coast to transport soy beans from plantations, via sea ports, to its growing population.

Demand for some resources is growing. For example, there are around five billion mobile phones on Earth, and the number is growing daily. A vital resource for these phones is a metal found in coltan rock, most of which is mined from the Congo rainforest. Mining is a huge growth industry in the boreal forest, too. With rising oil prices, areas of boreal forest in Canada are being destroyed in order to get to the oily soil in tar pit reserves hidden underneath.

Climate and Environment

Scientists warn that global warming, partly caused by deforestation worldwide, will create a bubble of heat in the atmosphere over South America. This will dry the climate over the region and cause water shortages in the region. Continuing destructive farming practices in converted forest lands could increase soil erosion and decrease soil fertility. This will make farming and ranching very difficult. Increasing forest fires, mining and other development could cause major pollution of both the atmosphere and water sources.

 Koala bears are just one forest species that is disappearing partly as a result of deforestation.

A Preferable Future

By 2050 forests could be in an even healthier state than in 2007. For this to happen, people around the world need to take responsibility as global citizens. Governments, charities, communities and individuals must work together to protect the remaining forests.

More reserves are urgently needed to make sure frontier forest survives and biodiversity is preserved. Degraded land needs to be carefully reforested with native species and multi-species plantations developed. Careful management can help to increase both biodiversity and timber production. Illegal logging can become a thing of the past if people demand more widespread forest certification and governments implement tougher laws to stop illegal trade in forest products.

◄ The Green Belt movement that started in Africa in the 1970s has transformed into a global drive for reforestation.

CASE STUDY
Plant a Billion Trees

In 1977, Wangari Maathai started to plant trees in Kenya because she was concerned about deforestation. Other people shared her ideas about planting native species to improve local environments and they started the Green Belt Movement, which by 2004 had planted 30 million trees in 12 African countries. Now the idea has gone global. The Plant for the Planet: Billion Tree Campaign encouraged people, communities, organisations, businesses and governments to plant at least one billion trees worldwide during 2007.

Paying for Change

It costs a lot to stop deforestation. Money is needed to set up reserves, to employ rangers and to educate people, from poor farmers to plantation owners, on how better to treat land, for example. One of the best ways by which poor countries have found the money to conserve forests is through Debt for Nature schemes. Many LEDCs owe money to MEDCS. This is often money they borrowed in the past to build expensive developments, such as powerplants. LEDCs struggle to pay off the debts, but one easy way to find money has been to grow cash crops on deforested land. However, governments of some MEDCs have decided to forget about the debts so long as the LEDCs spent the money instead on environmental protection.

Benefiting from Change

People living in and around forests should farm more sustainably. They can then benefit from the changes as soil fertility grows, water supplies increase and traditional ways of life continue. Fair trade organisations could help people in LEDCs to sell tropical forest crops for a fair price around the world. The spread of technologies could reduce wood use. For example, using cheap solar ovens to cook food reduces the need for fuelwood.

All of these changes will help the climate and benefit us all. With fewer trees burned, greenhouse gas emissions will fall and more atmospheric carbon dioxide will be taken in by trees, slowing global warming.

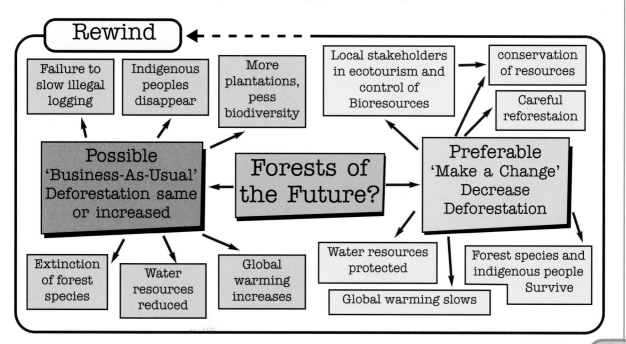

Glossary and Further Information

Acid rain Rain mixed with atmospheric pollution that is harmful to the environment.

Biofuel Fuel made from plants grown on plantations, agricultural by-products or from domestic or agricultural waste.

Bioresources Raw materials from living things used to make medicines.

Bushmeat Meat from wild animals.

Ecosystem A community of living things and the environment in which they live and interact.

Ecotourism Nature-based tourism that is ecologically sustainable.

Endangered In danger of dying out or becoming extinct owing to small populations and habitat under threat. Many forest species are endangered owing to deforestation.

Forest fragmentation The process of breaking up blocks of forest into smaller areas for example by creating roads or settlements.

Fuelwood Wood used primarily for heat or for conversion to other forms of energy.

Indigenous With origins in a region or country.

Native Originally growing or living in a particular area. For example, native Americans were the first inhabitants of North America and Scots pine trees are native plants to Scotland.

NTFPs Non-timber forest products such as nuts, spices and fuelwood.

Slash and burn A type of land clearance where people cut down plants and then burn the remains.

Sustainable Carried out without depleting or permanently damaging resources. Sustainable forestry is when people replant trees and manage woodland when they harvest timber and other products.

Transpiration The evaporation of water from leaf surfaces. This process drives the movement of water from the ground through trees.

Tuberculosis A lung disease that causes breathing problems.

Log On

http://kids.mongabay.com
A wealth of pictures and clear explanation of the many issues to do with tropical deforestation.

http://borealkids.org
Information on boreal forests, the creatures that live there and ways you can help preserve what is left.

www.unep.org/billiontreecampaign/about/index.asp
Log on to learn about the global reforestation movement.

Visit

The Woodland Trust
The Woodland Trust manages many UK woods you can visit. Log on to their website for details on how to find them: www.woodlandtrust.org.uk/woods/index.htm

The Eden Project
Visit the Eden project to walk through a rainforest biome. For more information, go to: www.edenproject.com/education/481.html

Read

Earthwatch: Saving the Rainforests
Sally Morgan (Franklin Watts, 2005)

21st Century Debates: Rainforests
Ewan McLeish (Wayland, 2003)

Green Alert: Vanishing Forests
Lim Cheung Puay (Raintree, 2004)

Biomes Atlases: Temperate Forests
John Woodward (Raintree, 2003)

Biomes Atlases: Taiga Trevor Day (Raintree, 2003)

Topic Web

Use this topic web to discover themes and ideas in subjects that are related to deforestation.

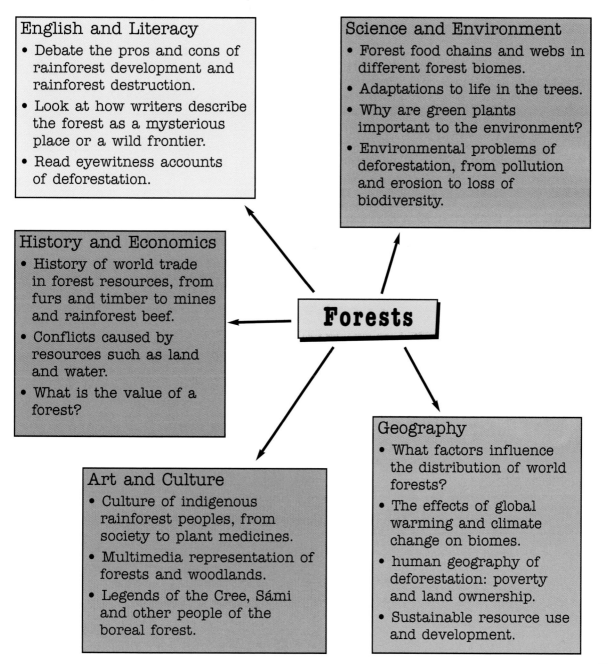

English and Literacy
- Debate the pros and cons of rainforest development and rainforest destruction.
- Look at how writers describe the forest as a mysterious place or a wild frontier.
- Read eyewitness accounts of deforestation.

Science and Environment
- Forest food chains and webs in different forest biomes.
- Adaptations to life in the trees.
- Why are green plants important to the environment?
- Environmental problems of deforestation, from pollution and erosion to loss of biodiversity.

History and Economics
- History of world trade in forest resources, from furs and timber to mines and rainforest beef.
- Conflicts caused by resources such as land and water.
- What is the value of a forest?

Forests

Art and Culture
- Culture of indigenous rainforest peoples, from society to plant medicines.
- Multimedia representation of forests and woodlands.
- Legends of the Cree, Sámi and other people of the boreal forest.

Geography
- What factors influence the distribution of world forests?
- The effects of global warming and climate change on biomes.
- human geography of deforestation: poverty and land ownership.
- Sustainable resource use and development.

Index